Veggie-Licious Low-Carb Recipes

Delicious, Low-Carb Vegetarian & Vegan Dishes for a Healthier You

Low Carb Recipes for Healthy Living

by

Josephine Ellise

© 2023 Josephine Ellise. All Rights Reserved

Copyright Notices

Do not make any print or electronic reproductions, sell, re-publish, or distribute this book in parts or as a whole unless you have express written consent from me or my team.

There. I said it. That's the most tedious part of cookbook writing or even reading… With that out of the way, we can get to the exciting stuff: cooking!

Before we move on, though, please don't take the copyright with a grain of salt. I put a lot of work into my books and like to protect them, otherwise I wouldn't even have copyrighted this book you're holding. Just keep it in mind and don't let others infringe on it either. Thanks, guys!

Table of Contents

Introduction 6

Appetizer Recipes 8

    1. Masala Pineapple 9

    2. Pea Olives 11

    3. Ham Swirls 13

    4. Cream Mushrooms 15

    5. Cajun Salamis 17

    6. Turnip Canapes 19

    7. Lettuce Mustard Rolls 21

    8. Potato Bites 23

    9. Bacon Jalapeños 25

    10. Tomato Boats 27

Soup Recipes 29

    11. Cabbage Garlic Soup 30

    12. Olive Lentil Soup 32

    13. Potato French Bean Soup 34

    14. Tofu Bell Pepper Soup 36

    15. Basil Bean Soup 38

16. Mushroom Cream Soup 40

17. Asparagus Leek Soup 42

18. Sweet Corn Soup 44

19. Green Onion Pumpkin Soup 46

20. Tomato Pepper Soup 48

Main Course Recipes 50

21. Mix Veg Quinoa 51

22. Stuffed and Baked Squash 53

23. Asparagus with Garlic Potatoes 55

24. Poblano Chili Mini Pizza 57

25. Soybean and Green Pea Curry 59

26. Stir-Fried Tofu with Veggies 61

27. Chickpea Casserole 63

28. Butter Basil Pasta with Sun-dried Tomatoes 65

29. Corn Stuffed Bell Pepper 67

30. Olive Stuffed Aubergine 69

Salad Recipes 71

31. Fruit Salad 72

32. Black Olive Spring Onion Salad 74

33. Peanut Nacho Salad 76

34. Cabbage Green Pea Salad 78

35. Red Cabbage Sun-dried Tomato Salad 80

36. Quinoa Potato Salad 82

37. Lentil Corn Salad 84

38. Baked Beans Green Onion Salad 86

39. Radish Carrot Salad 88

40. Turnip Bell Pepper Salad 90

Dessert Recipes 92

41. Lychee Popsicles 93

42. Fruit Cream 95

43. Ginger Cherries 97

44. Baked Cinnamon Pear 99

45. Pineapple Halwa 101

46. Crispy Kiwi Scramble 103

47. Carrot Pudding 105

48. Strawberry Pie 107

49. Baked Peach and Almond Mix 109

50. Coconut Date Bites 111

Author's Afterthoughts 114

Introduction

To prepare tasty, nutritious, and low-carb vegetarian meals, go no further than *"Veggie-Licious Low-Carb Dishes."* Ingredients for these dishes may be found at any grocery store and can be prepared quickly.

The delicious cuisine that may be enjoyed while adhering to a low-carb diet is a major perk. Getting rid of manufactured carbohydrates leaves you with complete, natural meals that are not only healthier but also simpler to prepare and enjoy. Vegetarians seeking the health advantages of a low-carbohydrate diet without losing flavor will find plenty to love in this cookbook. A low-carb diet may be helpful if you're trying to eat healthily and reduce excess body fat.

Find your ideal weight with the aid of this cookbook. There's something for everyone in this collection of 50 delicious dishes. You will find creative solutions to your hunger, whether you are a vegetarian, vegan, or on a low-carb diet. You may satisfy your sweet desire without gaining weight thanks to the easy and rapid preparation of the sweets.

Vegetarians and vegans on the Atkins plan might be envious of their carnivorous pals' rapid weight loss. The high-protein and low-carbohydrate composition of all the dishes makes it clear why this diet is effective. Nutritional support for the dieter's health may be found in the abundance of fresh fruits and vegetables included in the meals.

Consuming meat is not required to reap the benefits of a high-protein diet. Protein from plants can be just as healthy as that from animals. The plant-based proteins in foods like beans, lentils, quinoa, and tofu, for instance, are of the highest quality. You can easily meet your daily protein requirements without eating meat if you include these items in your diet.

This book is useful whether your goal is to shed pounds, ramp up your energy levels, or just feel better in general.

vvvvvvvvvvvvvvvvvvvvvvvvvvvvvvvvvv

Appetizer Recipes

1. Masala Pineapple

Makes: 4

Prep Time: 5 minutes

Cook Time: 10 minutes

Ingredient List

- 4 thick slices of pineapple
- Salt and chili powder, for seasoning according to personal preference

vvvvvvvvvvvvvvvvvvvvvvvvvvvvvvvvvvvvvv

Instructions

I. Preheat the oven to a temperature of 350°F.
II. Combine chili and salt in a bowl. Rub the mix onto both sides of each pineapple slice.
III. Now, place the pineapple over the oven's grill and bake them for a period of 10 minutes (turn the slices around once halfway through).
IV. Once done, remove the pineapple slices from the
V. Serve them hot!

2. Pea Olives

Makes: 10

Prep Time: 10 minutes

Cook Time: 0 minutes

Ingredient List

- 1 cup of mashed peas
- 10 green olives

vvvvvvvvvvvvvvvvvvvvvvvvvvvvvvvvvvvv

Instructions

I. Scoop out the pulp from each olive with the help of a skewer.
II. Then, stuff them with mashed peas.
III. Serve!

3. Ham Swirls

Makes: 4

Prep Time: 5 minutes

Cook Time: 10 minutes

Ingredient List

- 4 square slices of ham
- 1 cup of low-fat Parmesan cheese, grated
- 1/2 cup of corn kernels
- Salt and pepper, for seasoning

vvvvvvvvvvvvvvvvvvvvvvvvvvvvvvvvvv

Instructions

I. Preheat your oven to a temperature of 350°F.
II. Grease a baking tray with olive oil and keep it aside.
III. Combine all of the ingredients listed except for the ham in a bowl. Mix well.
IV. Place a ham slice over a chopping board and put 1/4 part of the prepared mix on one edge of the slice. Roll the edge with stuffing towards the other edge like a swirl.
V. Repeat the same procedure and make 3 more swirls.
VI. Now, place the swirls in the prepared baking tray and bake them for 10 minutes.
VII. Once done, remove the baking tray from the
VIII. Serve hot!

4. Cream Mushrooms

Makes: 10

Prep Time: 5 minutes

Cook Time: 10 minutes

Ingredient List

- 10 white button mushrooms, stems removed
- 1 cup of low-fat mozzarella cheese
- Salt and pepper, for seasoning according to personal preference

vvvvvvvvvvvvvvvvvvvvvvvvvvvvvvvvvvvv

Instructions

I. Preheat the oven to 350°F.
II. Lightly grease a baking tray with butter and keep it aside.
III. Combine cheese, salt, and pepper in a bowl. Mix well.
IV. Stuff the hollow side of the mushrooms with the prepared cheese mix.
V. Place the stuffed mushrooms in the prepared baking tray and bake them for a period of 10 minutes.
VI. Once done, remove the baking tray from the
VII. Serve hot!

5. Cajun Salamis

Makes: 8

Prep Time: 5 minutes

Cook Time: 10 minutes

Ingredient List

- 8 salamis
- 1 tsp. of Cajun spice
- 2 tbsp. of Greek yogurt
- Salt and pepper, for seasoning according to personal preference

vvvvvvvvvvvvvvvvvvvvvvvvvvvvvvvvv

Instructions

I. Preheat the oven to a temperature of 350°F.
II. Lightly grease a baking tray with olive oil and keep it aside.
III. Combine all of the ingredients listed in a bowl except for the salami and mix well.
IV. Then, add in salamis and evenly coat each salami with the prepared marination.
V. Refrigerate the salamis for a period of 4-5 hours (refrigerate overnight for best results).
VI. Now, place the marinated salamis on the prepared baking tray and bake them for a period of 10 minutes (turn them around once halfway through).
VII. Once done, remove the baking tray from the
VIII. Serve hot!

6. Turnip Canapes

Makes: 8

Prep Time: 5 minutes

Cook Time: 10 minutes

Ingredient List

- 2 large turnips, sliced into circular discs
- 1 cup of fat cream cheese
- A handful of mint leaves, finely chopped
- Salt and pepper, for seasoning according to personal preference

vvvvvvvvvvvvvvvvvvvvvvvvvvvvvvvvvvv

Instructions

I. Combine all of the ingredients listed in a bowl except for the turnips and mix well.
II. Then, top each turnip disc with the prepared mix.
III. Serve!

7. Lettuce Mustard Rolls

Makes: 4

Prep Time: 5 minutes

Cook Time: 0 minutes

Ingredient List

- 4 lettuce leaves
- 1 small onion, finely chopped
- 1 small tomato, finely chopped
- 4 tbsp. of mustard sauce
- Salt and pepper, for seasoning according to personal preference

vvvvvvvvvvvvvvvvvvvvvvvvvvvvvvvvvvv

Instructions

I. Combine all of the ingredients listed except for the lettuce leaf in a bowl. Mix well.
II. Place a lettuce leaf over a chopping board and put 1/4 part of the prepared mix on one edge of the leaf. Roll the edge with stuffing towards the other edge like a roll.
III. Repeat the same procedure and make 3 more rolls.
IV. Serve!

8. Potato Bites

Makes: 8

Prep Time: 5 minutes

Cook Time: 10 minutes

Ingredient List

- 1 large potato, sliced into circular discs
- 1 cup of cheddar cheese, grated
- 1 small onion, finely chopped
- 1 tsp. of fresh chives, chopped
- Salt and pepper, for seasoning according to personal preference

vvvvvvvvvvvvvvvvvvvvvvvvvvvvvvvvv

Instructions

I. Preheat the oven to a temperature of 350°F.
II. Lightly grease a baking tray with olive oil and keep it aside.
III. Combine all of the ingredients listed in a bowl except for the potato and mix well.
IV. Then, top each potato disc with the prepared mix.
V. Now, place the discs in the prepared baking tray and bake them for a period of 10 minutes.
VI. Once done, remove the baking tray from the
VII. Serve hot!

9. Bacon Jalapeños

Makes: 4

Prep Time: 5 minutes

Cook Time: 10 minutes

Ingredient List

- 4 jalapeno pepper
- 1 medium boiled potato, peeled and diced
- 4 bacon rashers
- Salt and pepper, for seasoning according to personal preference

vvvvvvvvvvvvvvvvvvvvvvvvvvvvvvvvvvvv

Instructions

I. Preheat the oven to a temperature of 350ºF.
II. Lightly grease a baking tray with olive oil and keep it aside.
III. Make a vertical pocket in each pepper and scoop out the seeds. Keep this aside
IV. Mash the potato in a bowl with a fork. Add in salt and pepper. Mix well.
V. Stuff the peppers with the prepared potato mix. Wrap each stuffed pepper with a bacon rasher and seal it with a toothpick
VI. Now, place the stuffed peppers on the prepared baking tray and bake them for a period of 10 minutes.
VII. Once done, remove the baking tray from the
VIII. Serve hot!

10. Tomato Boats

Makes: 8

Prep Time: 5 minutes

Cook Time: 15 minutes

Ingredient List

- 2 medium tomatoes, halved and deseeded
- 1 cup of low-fat cottage cheese, crumbled
- 1 small green bell pepper, finely chopped
- Salt and pepper, for seasoning according to personal preference

vvvvvvvvvvvvvvvvvvvvvvvvvvvvvvvvvv

Instructions

I. Preheat the oven to a temperature of 350°F.
II. Lightly grease a baking tray with olive oil and keep it aside.
III. Combine cheese, bell pepper, salt, and pepper in a bowl. Mix well.
IV. Stuff each half of the tomato with the prepared mix.
V. Now, place the stuffed tomatoes on the prepared baking tray and bake them for a period of 10-15 minutes.
VI. Once done, remove the baking tray from the
VII. Serve hot!

Soup Recipes

11. Cabbage Garlic Soup

Makes: 2

Prep Time: 15 minutes

Cook Time: 30 minutes

Ingredient List

- 4 cups of cabbage, chopped
- 2 spring onions, finely chopped
- 1 tsp. of dry garlic powder
- 1 cup of tomato puree
- 1-quart of vegetable stock
- 1 tbsp. of butter
- Salt, for seasoning according to personal preference

Instructions

I. Take all of the ingredients listed, grab a hold of a pan that has a deep bottom, place the ingredients in it and place it over a high flame.

II. Bring the mixture to a boil and cover the pan with a lid. Let it simmer over low heat until the liquid reduces to half.

III. Once ready, transfer the soup to two bowls.

IV. Serve hot!

12. Olive Lentil Soup

Makes: 2

Prep Time: 15 minutes

Cook Time: 30 minutes

Ingredient List

- 4 cups of cooked lentils
- 2 cups of black olives, halved
- 1 medium onion, finely chopped
- 1 tsp. of garlic paste
- 1 cup of tomato puree
- 1-quart of vegetable stock
- 1 tbsp. of butter
- Salt, for seasoning according to personal preference

Instructions

I. Take all of the ingredients listed, grab a hold of a deep bottom pan, add the ingredients to it and place it over a high flame.
II. Bring the mixture to a boil and cover the pan with a lid. Let it simmer over low heat until the liquid reduces to half.
III. Once ready, transfer the soup to two bowls.
IV. Serve hot!

13. Potato French Bean Soup

Makes: 2

Prep Time: 15 minutes

Cook Time: 30 minutes

Ingredient List

- 2 medium potatoes, diced
- 2 cups of french beans, chopped
- 2 spring onions, finely chopped
- 1/4 tsp. of nutmeg
- 1 cup of tomato puree
- 1-quart of vegetable stock
- 1 tbsp. of butter
- Salt, for seasoning according to personal preference

vvvvvvvvvvvvvvvvvvvvvvvvvvvvvvvvvvvvvv

Instructions

I. Take all of the ingredients listed, grab a hold of a pan that has a deep bottom, place the ingredients in it and place it over a high flame.

II. Bring the mixture to a boil and cover the pan with a lid. Let it simmer over low heat until the veggies are done and the liquid reduces to half.

III. Once ready, transfer the soup to two bowls.

IV. Serve hot!

14. Tofu Bell Pepper Soup

Makes: 2

Prep Time: 15 minutes

Cook Time: 30 minutes

Ingredient List

- 1/4 pound of firm tofu, diced
- 1 large bell pepper, finely chopped
- 1 medium onion, finely chopped
- 1 tsp. of ginger paste
- 1 cup of tomato puree
- 1-quart of vegetable stock
- 1 tbsp. of butter
- Salt, for seasoning according to personal preference

Instructions

I. Take all of the ingredients listed, grab a hold of a pan that has a deep bottom, place the ingredients in it and place it over a high flame.

II. Bring the mixture to a boil and cover the pan with a lid. Let it simmer over low heat until the liquid reduces to half.

III. Once ready, transfer the soup to two bowls.

IV. Serve hot!

15. Basil Bean Soup

Makes: 2

Prep Time: 15 minutes

Cook Time: 30 minutes

Ingredient List

- 4 cups of baked beans
- 2 cups of fresh basil leaves
- 1 medium onion, finely chopped
- 1 tsp. of garlic paste
- 1 cup of tomato puree
- 1-quart vegetable stock
- 1 tbsp. of butter
- Salt, for seasoning according to personal preference

VVVVVVVVVVVVVVVVVVVVVVVVVVVVVVVVVVVV

Instructions

I. Take all of the ingredients listed, grab a hold of a pan that has a deep bottom, place the ingredients in it and place it over a high flame.
II. Bring the mixture to a boil and cover the pan with a lid. Let it simmer over low heat until the liquid reduces to half.
III. Once ready, transfer the soup to two bowls.
IV. Serve hot!

16. Mushroom Cream Soup

Makes: 2

Prep Time: 15 minutes

Cook Time: 30 minutes

Ingredient List

- 1/4 pound of white button mushrooms, chopped
- 1 cup of low-fat sour cream
- 1 medium onion, finely chopped
- 1 tsp. of fresh chives
- 1 cup of tomato puree
- 1-quart of vegetable stock
- 1 tbsp. of butter
- Salt, for seasoning according to personal preference

Instructions

I. Take all of the ingredients listed, grab a hold of a pan that has a deep bottom, place the ingredients in it and place it over a high flame.

II. Bring the mixture to a boil and cover the pan with a lid. Let it simmer over low heat until the mushrooms are cooked through and the liquid reduces to half.

III. Once ready, transfer the soup to two bowls.

IV. Serve hot!

17. Asparagus Leek Soup

Makes: 2

Prep Time: 15 minutes

Cook Time: 30 minutes

Ingredient List

- 1/4 pound of asparagus, chopped
- 1 medium leek, chopped
- 1/2 tsp. of dried rosemary, ground
- 1 cup of tomato puree
- 1-quart of vegetable stock
- 1 tbsp. of butter
- Salt, for seasoning according to personal preference

Instructions

I. Take all of the ingredients listed, grab a hold of a pan that has a deep bottom, place the ingredients in it and place it over a high flame.

II. Bring the mixture to a boil and cover the pan with a lid. Let it simmer over low heat until the veggies have cooked through and the liquid reduces to half.

III. Once ready, transfer the soup to two bowls.

IV. Serve hot!

18. Sweet Corn Soup

Makes: 2

Prep Time: 15 minutes

Cook Time: 30 minutes

Ingredient List

- 2 cups of corn kernels
- 1/4 pound of baby corn, chopped
- 1 medium onion, finely chopped
- 1 tsp. of soy sauce
- 1 cup of tomato puree
- 1-quart of vegetable stock
- 1 tsp. of raw honey
- 1 tbsp. of butter
- Salt, for seasoning according to personal preference

Instructions

I. Take all of the ingredients listed, grab a hold of a pan that has a deep bottom, place the ingredients in it and place it over a high flame.
II. Bring the mixture to a boil and cover the pan with a lid. Let it simmer over low heat until the liquid reduces to half.
III. Once ready, transfer the soup to two bowls.
IV. Serve hot!

19. Green Onion Pumpkin Soup

Makes: 2

Prep Time: 15 minutes

Cook Time: 30 minutes

Ingredient List

- 1/4 pound of pumpkin, chopped
- 2-3 green onions, chopped
- 1/2 tsp. of pumpkin spice
- 1 cup of tomato puree
- 1-quart of vegetable stock
- 1 tbsp. of butter
- Salt, for seasoning according to personal preference

vvvvvvvvvvvvvvvvvvvvvvvvvvvvvvvvvvvvvv

Instructions

I. Take all of the ingredients listed, grab a hold of a pan that has a deep bottom, place the ingredients in it and place it over a high flame.
II. Bring the mixture to a boil and cover the pan with a lid. Let it simmer over low heat until the veggies have cooked through and the liquid reduces to half.
III. Once ready, transfer the soup to two bowls.
IV. Serve hot!

20. Tomato Pepper Soup

Makes: 2

Prep Time: 15 minutes

Cook Time: 30 minutes

Ingredient List

- 1 cups of sun dried tomatoes
- 2 cups of black olives, halved
- 1 medium onion, finely chopped
- 1/2 tsp. of peppercorn, ground
- 2 cups of tomato puree
- 1-quart of vegetable stock
- 1 tbsp. of butter
- Salt, for seasoning according to personal preference

Instructions

I. Take all of the ingredients listed, grab a hold of a pan that has a deep bottom, place the ingredients in it and place it over a high flame.

II. Bring the mixture to a boil and cover the pan with a lid. Let it simmer over low heat until the liquid reduces to half.

III. Once ready, transfer the soup to two bowls.

IV. Serve hot!

Main Course Recipes

21. Mix Veg Quinoa

Makes: 2

Prep Time: 15 minutes

Cook Time: 45 minutes

Ingredient List

- 3 cups of quinoa, rinsed
- 1 medium onion, finely chopped
- 1 tsp. of garlic paste
- 1 tsp. of ginger paste
- 1 cup of tomato puree
- 1 cup of carrots, finely chopped
- 1 cup of green peas
- Florets of 1 small head of broccoli
- 6 cups of water
- 1 tsp. of curry powder
- 2 tbsp. of olive oil
- Salt, for seasoning according to personal preference

vvvvvvvvvvvvvvvvvvvvvvvvvvvvvvvv

Instructions

I. Heat the olive oil in a deep bottom pan over a medium-high flame. Add in the onion and cook until it turns golden-brown. Then, add the garlic paste and ginger. Cook these ingredients for a minute.
II. Add in tomato puree and cook until all of the ingredients listed turn into a thick gravy.
III. Now, add the curry powder and salt. Mix well and cook them for a minute.
IV. Then, add in the rest of the ingredients listed and cover the pan with its lid. Let the mixture simmer over low heat until the veggies and quinoa are cooked through and the water has evaporated
V. Once done, transfer the quinoa to a serving bowl.
VI. Serve hot!

22. Stuffed and Baked Squash

Makes: 2

Prep Time: 10 minutes

Cook Time: 30 minutes

Ingredient List

- 1 medium butternut squash, halved
- 1 large onion, finely chopped
- 1 large tomato, finely chopped
- 1 cup mozzarella cheese, grated
- 2 tbsp. of olive oil
- Salt and pepper, for seasoning according to personal preference

Instructions

I. Preheat the oven to a temperature of 350°F.
II. Lightly grease a baking tray with some olive oil spray and keep it aside.
III. Scoop out the pulp from each half of the squash, and keep the squash shell 1/2 thick. Keep the shells aside and mash the pulp with the help of a fork until smooth. Keep this aside.
IV. Heat olive oil in a large non-stick pan over a medium-high flame. Stir in the onion and sauté until it is golden brown, add in the tomato, and cook until it turns into a thick gravy.
V. Then, add in the squash pulp, salt, and pepper and cook it for a period of 5 minutes while stirring occasionally.
VI. Once done, stuff the squash shells with the cooked mix and top them with mozzarella cheese. Place them on the prepared baking tray.
VII. Bake them for a period of 10-15 minutes.
VIII. Serve hot!

23. Asparagus with Garlic Potatoes

Makes: 2

Prep Time: 15 minutes

Cook Time: 15 minutes

Ingredient List

- A bunch of boiled asparagus, halved
- 2-3 spring onions, finely chopped
- 2 medium onions, boiled and peeled
- 2 tsp. of garlic paste
- 1 tsp. of ginger paste
- 1 tsp. of Cajun spice
- 2 tbsp. of olive oil
- Salt, for seasoning according to personal preference

Instructions

I. Heat olive oil in a large non-stick pan over a medium-high flame. Add in the onion and cook until they are translucent. Then, add in Cajun spice, salt, and pepper. Cook the mixture for a minute and remove the pan from the Keep it aside.

II. Put the potatoes in a bowl and mash them with a fork until smooth. Add in garlic, salt, and pepper. Mix well.

III. Once done, serve the asparagus with mashed potatoes on the

IV. Serve hot!

24. Poblano Chili Mini Pizza

Makes: 8-10

Prep Time: 10 minutes

Cook Time: 15 minutes

Ingredient List

- 4-5 poblano chili, halved and deseeded
- 1 large onion, chopped finely
- 1 large tomato, finely chopped
- 1 cup of mozzarella cheese, grated
- 1/2 tsp. of oregano
- 1/4 tsp. of chili flakes
- Salt, for seasoning according to personal preference

vvvvvvvvvvvvvvvvvvvvvvvvvvvvvvvvvvv

Instructions

I. Preheat the oven to a temperature of 350°F.
II. Grease a baking tray lightly with some olive oil spray and keep it aside.
III. Combine the onion, tomatoes, mozzarella cheese, oregano, chili flakes, and salt in a bowl. Mix well.
IV. Once done, stuff the poblano with the prepared mix and place them on the baking tray.
V. Bake them for a period of 10-15 minutes.
VI. Serve hot!

25. Soybean and Green Pea Curry

Makes: 2

Prep Time: 15 minutes

Cook Time: 45 minutes

Ingredient List

- 2 cups of boiled soybean
- 2 cups of green pea kernels
- 1 medium onion, finely chopped
- 1 tsp. of garlic paste
- 1 tsp. of ginger paste
- 1 cup of tomato puree
- 1 1/2 quart of water
- 1 tsp. of curry powder
- 2 tbsp. of olive oil
- Salt, for seasoning according to personal preference

vvvvvvvvvvvvvvvvvvvvvvvvvvvvvvvvvv

Instructions

I. Heat olive oil over a sauté mode. Add in the onion and cook until they are golden-brown. Then, add in the ginger and garlic paste. Cook this for a minute.

II. Add in the tomato puree and cook until all of the ingredients listed turn into a thick gravy.

III. Now, add the curry powder, soybean, green peas, salt, and water.

IV. Cover the pan with a lid and let it simmer over low heat until the liquid reduces to 1/4.

V. Once done, transfer the curry to a serving bowl.

VI. Serve hot with boiled rice!

26. Stir-Fried Tofu with Veggies

Makes: 2

Prep Time: 20 minutes

Cook Time: 20 minutes

Ingredient List

- 1/2 pound of firm tofu
- 2-3 spring onions, finely chopped
- 1 large red bell pepper, chopped
- 2 cups of cabbage, finely chopped
- 2 cups of carrots, julienne
- 2 cups of french beans, chopped
- 2 tsp. of soy sauce
- 1 tbsp. of white vinegar
- 1/2 tbsp. of red chili sauce
- 1 tbsp. of honey
- 2 tbsp. of coconut oil
- Salt and pepper, for seasoning according to personal preference

vvvvvvvvvvvvvvvvvvvvvvvvvvvvvvvvv

Instructions

I. Heat oil in a large non-stick pan over a medium-high flame. Add in all of the veggies and tofu. Cook them for a few minutes

II. Then, add in the soy sauce, vinegar, chili sauce, salt, and pepper. Cover the pan with a lid and let it simmer over low heat until the veggies are cooked through while stirring occasionally.

III. Once cooked, add in honey and mix well.

IV. Remove the pan from the heat.

V. Serve hot!

27. Chickpea Casserole

Makes: 4

Prep Time: 10 minutes

Cook Time: 30 minutes

Ingredient List

- 5 cups of boiled chickpeas
- 3-4 spring onions, finely chopped
- 2 cups of cherry tomatoes, halved
- 3 cups of parsley leaves
- 1 cup of mozzarella cheese, grated
- Salt and pepper, for seasoning according to personal preference

Instructions

I. Preheat the oven to a temperature of 350°F.
II. Lightly grease a baking tray with some olive oil spray and keep it aside.
III. Combine all of the ingredients listed in a large bowl and put them on the prepared baking tray.
IV. Bake them for a period of 20-30 minutes.
V. Serve hot!

28. Butter Basil Pasta with Sun-dried Tomatoes

Makes: 2

Prep Time: 10 minutes

Cook Time: 15 minutes

Ingredient List

- 1/2 pound of scooped out squash spaghetti
- 1 large onion, finely chopped
- 2 cups of sun-dried tomatoes
- 2 tbsp. of butter
- 1/2 cup of low fat heavy cream
- A handful of fresh basil leaves
- Salt and pepper, for seasoning according to personal preference

vvvvvvvvvvvvvvvvvvvvvvvvvvvvvvvvvv

Instructions

I. Heat olive oil in a large non-stick pan over a medium-high flame. Stir in the onion and sauté them until they are translucent. Add in the tomatoes, basil, salt, and pepper. Cook them for a few minutes.

II. Then, add in the spaghetti and heavy cream. Cover the pan with a lid and let it simmer over low heat for a period of 5-10 minutes while stirring occasionally.

III. Once done, remove the pan from the heat.

IV. Serve hot!

29. Corn Stuffed Bell Pepper

Makes: 2

Prep Time: 10 minutes

Cook Time: 15 minutes

Ingredient List

- 2 medium onion, finely chopped
- 2 cups of corn kernels
- 1 cup of mozzarella cheese, grated
- 1 cup of tomato puree
- 1 tsp. of Cajun spice
- Salt and pepper, for seasoning according to personal preference

vvvvvvvvvvvvvvvvvvvvvvvvvvvvvvv

Instructions

I. Begin the cooking process by preheating the oven to a temperature of 350°F.

II. Lightly grease a baking tray with some olive oil spray and keep it aside.

III. Combine the corn, cheese, tomato puree, Cajun spice, salt, and pepper in a bowl. Mix the ingredients together well and stuff the bell peppers with the prepared corn mix. Place them on the prepared baking tray.

IV. Bake them for a period of 10-15 minutes.

V. Serve hot!

30. Olive Stuffed Aubergine

Makes: 2

Prep Time: 10 minutes

Cook Time: 30 minutes

Ingredient List

- 1 large aubergine, halved (length-ways)
- 1 cup of black olives, chopped
- 1 cup of green peas
- 1 tsp. of dried rosemary, ground
- 2 tbsp. of olive oil
- Salt and pepper, for seasoning according to personal preference

vvvvvvvvvvvvvvvvvvvvvvvvvvvvvvv

Instructions

I. Preheat the oven to a temperature of 350°F.
II. Lightly grease a baking tray with some olive oil spray and keep it aside.
III. Scoop out the pulp from each half of the aubergine, and keep the squash shell 1/2 thick. Keep the shells aside and mash the pulp with the help of a fork until smooth. Keep this aside.
IV. Heat olive oil in a large non-stick pan over a medium-high flame. Stir in the olives and peas. Cook them for a few minutes, while stirring occasionally.
V. Then, add in the aubergine pulp, rosemary, salt, and pepper. Cook this for a period of 5 minutes while stirring occasionally.
VI. Once done, stuff the aubergine shells with the cooked mix and top them with mozzarella cheese. Place them on the prepared baking tray.
VII. Bake them for a period of 10-15 minutes.
VIII. Serve hot!

Salad Recipes

31. Fruit Salad

Makes: 2

Prep Time: 15 minutes

Cook Time: 0 minutes

Ingredient List

- 1 cup of strawberries, hulled and chopped
- 1 cup of pineapple, finely chopped
- 1 cup of cherries, deseeded
- 1 cup of grapes, halved
- 1 cup of apple, chopped
- 1 tbsp. of lemon grass, finely chopped
- Juice of 1 lemon
- Salt, for seasoning according to personal preference

vvvvvvvvvvvvvvvvvvvvvvvvvvvvvvvvvvvvvv

Instructions

I. Put all of the ingredients listed in a large bowl and mix well.
II. Once ready, transfer the salad to two bowls.
III. Serve!

32. Black Olive Spring Onion Salad

Makes: 2

Prep Time: 15 minutes

Cook Time: 0 minutes

Ingredient List

- 2 cups of black olives, chopped
- 2-3 spring onions, finely chopped
- 1 head of lettuce, finely chopped
- A handful of fresh parsley leaves
- 2 tbsp. of low-fat cream cheese
- Salt and pepper, for seasoning according to personal preference

vvvvvvvvvvvvvvvvvvvvvvvvvvvvvvvvvvvvv

Instructions

I. Put all of the ingredients listed in a large bowl and mix well.
II. Once ready, transfer the salad to two bowls.
III. Serve!

33. Peanut Nacho Salad

Makes: 2

Prep Time: 15 minutes

Cook Time: 0 minutes

Ingredient List

- 2 cups of roasted peanuts
- 1/4 pound of nachos
- 2 spring onions, finely chopped
- 1 head of lettuce, finely chopped
- 1 cup of guacamole
- Salt and pepper, for seasoning according to personal preference

vvvvvvvvvvvvvvvvvvvvvvvvvvvvvvvvvvvv

Instructions

I. Put all of the ingredients listed in a large bowl and mix well.
II. Once ready, transfer the salad to two bowls.
III. Serve!

34. Cabbage Green Pea Salad

Makes: 2

Prep Time: 15 minutes

Cook Time: 0 minutes

Ingredient List

- 2 cups of boiled green pea kernels
- 1 small head of cabbage, chopped
- 2 spring onions, finely chopped
- 1/2 cup of Greek yogurt
- Salt and pepper, for seasoning according to personal preference

vvvvvvvvvvvvvvvvvvvvvvvvvvvvvvvvvvvv

Instructions

I. Put all of the ingredients listed in a large bowl and mix well.
II. Once ready, transfer the salad to two bowls.
III. Serve!

35. Red Cabbage Sun-dried Tomato Salad

Makes: 2

Prep Time: 15 minutes

Cook Time: 0 minutes

Ingredient List

- 2 cups of sun-dried tomatoes
- 1 small head of red cabbage, chopped
- 2 spring onions, finely chopped
- 1 tbsp. of Tahini
- Salt and pepper, for seasoning according to personal preference

vvvvvvvvvvvvvvvvvvvvvvvvvvvvvvvvvvvvv

Instructions

I. Put all of the ingredients listed in a large bowl and mix well.
II. Once ready, transfer the salad to two bowls.
III. Serve!

36. Quinoa Potato Salad

Makes: 2

Prep Time: 15 minutes

Cook Time: 0 minutes

Ingredient List

- 2 cups of roasted quinoa
- 1/4 pound of boiled salad potatoes, halved
- 2 spring onions, finely chopped
- 1 head of lettuce, finely chopped
- 1 tbsp. of teriyaki sauce
- Salt and pepper, for seasoning according to personal preference

vvvvvvvvvvvvvvvvvvvvvvvvvvvvvvvvvvvvvv

Instructions

I. Put all of the ingredients listed in a large bowl and mix well.
II. Once ready, transfer the salad to two bowls.
III. Serve!

37. Lentil Corn Salad

Makes: 2

Prep Time: 15 minutes

Cook Time: 0 minutes

Ingredient List

- 2 cups of boiled lentils
- 2 cups of corn kernels
- 1/4 pound of nachos
- 2 spring onions, finely chopped
- 1 head of lettuce, finely chopped
- 1 tbsp. of balsamic vinegar
- Salt and pepper, for seasoning according to personal preference

vvvvvvvvvvvvvvvvvvvvvvvvvvvvvvvvvvvvvv

Instructions

I. Put all of the ingredients listed in a large bowl and mix well.
II. Once ready, transfer the salad to two bowls.
III. Serve!

38. Baked Beans Green Onion Salad

Makes: 2

Prep Time: 15 minutes

Cook Time: 0 minutes

Ingredient List

- 3 cups of baked beans
- 2 green onions, finely chopped
- 1 head of lettuce, finely chopped
- 1 cup of hummus
- Salt and pepper, for seasoning according to personal preference

vvvvvvvvvvvvvvvvvvvvvvvvvvvvvvvvvvvvv

Instructions

I. Put all of the ingredients listed in a large bowl and mix well.
II. Once ready, transfer the salad to two bowls.
III. Serve!

39. Radish Carrot Salad

Makes: 2

Prep Time: 15 minutes

Cook Time: 0 minutes

Ingredient List

- 1/4 pound of radish, chopped
- 1/4 pound of carrots, chopped
- 2 spring onions, finely chopped
- 1 head of lettuce, finely chopped
- 1 tbsp. of low-fat french dressing
- Salt and pepper, for seasoning according to personal preference

vvvvvvvvvvvvvvvvvvvvvvvvvvvvvvvvvvvvvvv

Instructions

I. Put all of the ingredients listed in a large bowl and mix well.
II. Once ready, transfer the salad to two bowls.
III. Serve!

40. Turnip Bell Pepper Salad

Makes: 2

Prep Time: 15 minutes

Cook Time: 0 minutes

Ingredient List

- 1/4 pound of turnips, finely chopped
- 1 large red bell pepper, finely chopped
- 2 spring onions, finely chopped
- 1 head of lettuce, finely chopped
- 1 tbsp. of low fat mayonnaise
- Salt and pepper, for seasoning according to personal preference

vvvvvvvvvvvvvvvvvvvvvvvvvvvvvvvvvvvv

Instructions

I. Put all of the ingredients listed in a large bowl and mix them together well.
II. Once ready, transfer the salad to two bowls.
III. Serve!

Dessert Recipes

41. Lychee Popsicles

Makes: 4

Prep Time: 15 minutes

Cook Time: 0 minutes

Ingredient List

- 1/2 pound of lychee, peeled and deseeded
- 4 cups of skimmed milk
- 1/2 cup of rice malt

vvvvvvvvvvvvvvvvvvvvvvvvvvvvvvvvvvv

Instructions

I. Put all of the ingredients listed in a food processor and blend until smooth.
II. Pour the mix into the 4 Popsicle molds
III. Refrigerate it for a period of 4-5 hours.
IV. Serve the lychee popsicles chilled!

42. Fruit Cream

Makes: 2

Prep Time: 15 minutes

Cook Time: 0 minutes

Ingredient List

- 1 cup of strawberries, hulled and chopped
- 1 cup of pineapple, finely chopped
- 1 cup of cherries, deseeded
- 1 cup of grapes, halved
- 1 cup of apple, chopped
- 1/2 cup of low-fat cream cheese

Instructions

I. Put all of the ingredients listed in a large bowl. Mix well.
II. Once ready, transfer the fruit cream to two bowls.
III. Serve the fruit cream and enjoy it!

43. Ginger Cherries

Makes: 2

Prep Time: 5 minutes

Cook Time: 15 minutes

Ingredient List

- 1/2 pound of cherries, deseeded
- 2 tbsp. of freshly grated ginger
- 4 tsp. of rice malt

vvvvvvvvvvvvvvvvvvvvvvvvvvvvvvvvvv

Instructions

I. Preheat the oven to a temperature of 350°F.
II. Lightly grease a baking tray with the butter spray and keep it aside.
III. Put all of the ingredients listed in a large bowl. Mix well.
IV. Then, transfer the mix to the prepared baking dish in an even layer.
V. Bake it for a period of 10-15 minutes.
VI. Serve the ginger cherries warm.

44. Baked Cinnamon Pear

Makes: 2

Prep Time: 5 minutes

Cook Time: 15 minutes

Ingredient List

- 1/2 pound of pears, thinly sliced
- 1/4 tsp. of cinnamon
- 2 tsp. of raw honey

vvvvvvvvvvvvvvvvvvvvvvvvvvvvvvvvvvv

Instructions

I. Preheat the oven to a temperature of 350°F.
II. Lightly grease a baking tray with some olive oil spray and keep it aside.
III. Put the pears and cinnamon in a large bowl. Mix well.
IV. Then, transfer the mix to the prepared baking tray in a thin layer.
V. Bake this for a period of 10-15 minutes.
VI. Once ready, remove the baking tray from the oven and drizzle raw honey over the baked pear slices.
VII. Serve the baked cinnamon pear hot!

45. Pineapple Halwa

Makes: 2

Prep Time: 5 minutes

Cook Time: 15 minutes

Ingredient List

- 1/2 pound of pineapple, finely chopped
- 2 tsp. of pineapple essence
- 2 tbsp. of low fat unsalted butter

vvvvvvvvvvvvvvvvvvvvvvvvvvvvvvvvv

Instructions

I. Melt the butter in a non-stick pan over medium-high heat. Put all of the ingredients listed in it.

II. Cook the ingredients until the liquid evaporates completely.

III. Once ready, remove the pan from the

IV. Serve the pineapple halwa hot!

46. Crispy Kiwi Scramble

Makes: 2

Prep Time: 5 minutes

Cook Time: 15 minutes

Ingredient List

- 1/2 pound of kiwi, chopped
- 1 cup of rolled oats
- 6 tsp. of rice malt
- 1/4 tsp. of nutmeg
- Butter for greasing

vvvvvvvvvvvvvvvvvvvvvvvvvvvvvvvv

Instructions

I. Preheat the oven to a temperature of 350°F.
II. Lightly grease a baking dish with some butter and keep it aside.
III. Put all of the ingredients listed in a large bowl. Mix well.
IV. Then, transfer the mix to the prepared baking tray in an even layer.
V. Bake this for a period of 10-15 minutes.
VI. Once ready, remove the baking tray.
VII. Serve the crispy kiwi scramble hot!

47. Carrot Pudding

Makes: 2

Prep Time: 5 minutes

Cook Time: 45 minutes

Ingredient List

- 1/2 pound of carrots, grated
- 1 quart of skimmed milk
- 1/2 cup of rice malt
- 1/4 tsp. of cardamom powder

vvvvvvvvvvvvvvvvvvvvvvvvvvvvvvvvvvv

Instructions

I. Put all of the ingredients listed in a deep bottom pan except for the rice malt and place it over medium-high heat.
II. Cook the ingredients until the milk evaporates completely.
III. Once ready, remove the pan from the
IV. Serve the carrot pudding hot!

48. Strawberry Pie

Makes: 2

Prep Time: 5 minutes

Cook Time: 15 minutes

Ingredient List

- 1/2 pound of strawberries, hulled and chopped
- 2 cups of oatmeal
- 1 cup of flax meal
- 1 cup of milk
- 1 tsp. of vanilla essence
- 1 tsp. of baking powder
- 10 tsp. of rice malt

Instructions

I. Preheat the oven to a temperature of 350°F.
II. Lightly grease a baking dish with some butter and keep it aside.
III. Put all of the ingredients listed in a large bowl. Mix well.
IV. Then, transfer the mix to the prepared baking dish in an even layer.
V. Bake this for a period of 25-30 minutes or until the skewer inserted in the center comes out clean
VI. Once ready, remove the baking dish from the oven and make slices from the pie.
VII. Serve the strawberry pie warm!

49. Baked Peach and Almond Mix

Makes: 2

Prep Time: 5 minutes

Cook Time: 15 minutes

Ingredient List

- 1/2 pound of peaches, thinly sliced
- 2 cups of almonds, roughly chopped
- 4 tsp. of rice malt

vvvvvvvvvvvvvvvvvvvvvvvvvvvvvvvvv

Instructions

I. Preheat the oven to a temperature of 350°F.
II. Take some butter or cooking spray, and lightly grease a baking tray and keep it aside.
III. Put all of the ingredients listed in a large bowl. Mix well.
IV. Then, transfer the mix to the prepared baking dish in an even layer.
V. Bake this for a period of 10-15 minutes.
VI. Once ready, remove the baking dish from the
VII. Serve the baked peach and almond mix hot!

50. Coconut Date Bites

Makes: 2

Prep Time: 5 minutes

Cook Time: 15 minutes

Ingredient List

- 1/4 pound of dates
- 2 cups of desiccated coconut
- 2 tbsp. of rice malt

vvvvvvvvvvvvvvvvvvvvvvvvvvvvvvvvvvvv

Instructions

I. Put all of the ingredients listed in a food processor and blend until smooth.
II. Transfer the mix to a bowl and make 10 equal balls.
III. Serve the coconut date bites and enjoy!

Author Biography

Josephine has 4 kids. That means she's a full-time mom who has to cater to difficult flavor requirements and phases sometimes... Her twins don't like mushy foods, her daughter is lactose intolerant, and her son won't eat anything that doesn't have melted nacho cheese on it. In a nutshell, cooking was a nightmare for her. She still did it extremely lovingly, but there's no denying that cooking with so many conditions is difficult. Oh, and let's not forget that cooking for children also requires an art degree because if the food doesn't look fun, inferesting, or yummy there's no way they'll eat it!

At one point, Josephine considered giving in to the frozen food aisle and living off boxed chicken nuggets and frozen lasagna and vegan key-lime pie. However, the thought was quickly chased out of her imagination every time she swiped her card at the supermarket. It was over $350 in groceries every week! She had to do something about it otherwise she'd be broke in a month!

Thus, Josephine started looking into quick and healthy recipes that checked all her children's boxes without breaking the bank either. Within a matter of weeks, her children began to love their mom's home cooking more than ever and even began to open themselves up to new ingredients! After giving it some thought, she decided to start publishing her recipes, hoping to help some moms through picky eating phases and allergies. As long as you don't give in to frozen foods, her recipes will change the way you cook so much you'll actually enjoy it again!

Author's Afterthoughts

thank you

Being a single mother never quite gets "easy", but it's an especially entertaining and complicated feat when they're young. My kiddos are like bouncy balls that have been charged with endless energy. They're here, they're there, they're everywhere! While I have gotten used to all of our adventures, I definitely have to take a moment to thank you for supporting my work.

Not only does it allow me to spend more time with my kids, but it also helps me pay the bills and continue funding new cookbook projects as a single mom. Cooking for my kids during their picky eating phases is always tricky, but thankfully I have you to support me so I can get creative in the kitchen and solve their cravings and your life with all of my recipes.

Just hang in there because it's only a matter of time before my next book comes out, but until then, I'd really like it if you could share your thoughts about my recipes with me. Also, what kind of recipes would you like to see more of? School lunches? Meals for certain allergies? Whatever you come up with will benefit all the moms out there (including myself) who struggle to think of delicious healthy meals our kids will actually eat.

Keep me posted!

Josephine Ellis.

Printed in Poland
by Amazon Fulfillment
Poland Sp. z o.o., Wrocław
20 June 2023

a1031815-7f9f-42d1-ab06-a473738d7c6fR01